MW01070203

LEONARDO DA VINCI IN 30 SECONDS

About this book
... in 60 seconds

Leonardo da Vinci (1452—1519) was truly amazing. Skilled in many different areas, he created one of the most famous paintings of all time, the *Mona Lisa*, invented flying machines, planned towns, designed buildings, made maps, created musical instruments, studied geology, became an expert in human anatomy, and much, much more.

Leonardo was born in 15th-century Italy in a period known as the Renaissance, which means "rebirth." During this time, people rediscovered the teachings of the ancient Greeks and Romans and, building on this knowledge, made incredible advances in many areas, in particular in art, philosophy, and science. The Renaissance began in Italy and spread across Europe, fueled by great minds like Leonardo and great inventions such as Johannes Gutenberg's printing press.

However, it was a troubled time, too. Italy was not a unified country and wealthy rival families fought for power and influence. Despite this, the arts flourished, and artists such as Leonardo enjoyed the protection and support of wealthy people.

Unfortunately, for all his productivity, not much of Leonardo's work survives today, but we do know a lot about what he thought and imagined. This is because he wrote pages and pages of notes. There are manuscripts full of designs for amazing machines, clever inventions, and sketches and ideas for paintings. Leonardo recorded everything in his notebooks—even his shopping lists!

This book explores the mind and work of Leonardo da Vinci. Each chapter shows you a different aspect of this fascinating man, and explains what he thought about, experimented with, and created.

Every topic has a page you can read in 30 seconds and a quick sum-up you can read in just 3 seconds. There are also 3-minute missions where you can put your knowledge into use, from making your own paints to creating a self-powered vehicle.

So, put on your thinking cap and get ready to go on a voyage of discovery with one of the most creative geniuses of all time.

The man and his times

Leonardo da Vinci was a truly extraordinary man living in extraordinary times. Born during the explosion of artistic and scientific knowledge of the Renaissance, he was able to use his genius to rise from humble beginnings to become one of the most famous artists of all time. From his days as an artist's apprentice to his employment by one of the most important families in Italy, we can see how Leonardo made his mark on history.

The man and his times
Glossary

apprentice A young person who learned the essentials of his or her craft under a **master**.

commission When a person orders a painting or artwork from an artist, and arranges to pay him or her when the work is complete.

Gutenberg's printing press Invented in about 1450, this press used movable metal pieces to create type and revolutionized the process of printing books.

guild An organization that regulates a group of tradespeople, for example, bakers, shoemakers, or barbers. Guild membership was strictly controlled, as was the quality of the guild members' work.

invasion An attack by armed forces, often sent by one region or country, on a different country or region.

journal A record, which is usually written every day, of events in a person's life, as well as their ideas and observations.

Latin The language of ancient Rome, which continued to be used in the Middle Ages for law, government, and education.

lawyer A person who studied law at a university, and who is responsible for drawing up agreements, marriage contracts, and wills.

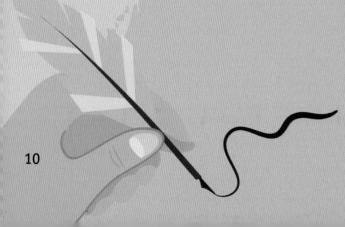

master A skilled craftsperson or artist who undertakes the training of apprentices.

quill A kind of pen used in Leonardo's day, which was made out of a bird's feather with the tip cut into a point. Goose feathers were most commonly used.

Renaissance A period of European history between the 14th and 17th centuries, when there were great advances in art, literature, education, exploration, and thinking.

sculpture Shaping wood, metal, stone, or other materials to make **three-dimensional** forms, such as human or animal figures.

skill The ability, often the result of practice and learning, to perform a task in the best possible way.

state A territory that is organized and ruled by a single government and set of laws.

technique The way in which an artist uses their **skill** and experience.

three-dimensional An object with height, width, and depth, like objects in the real world.

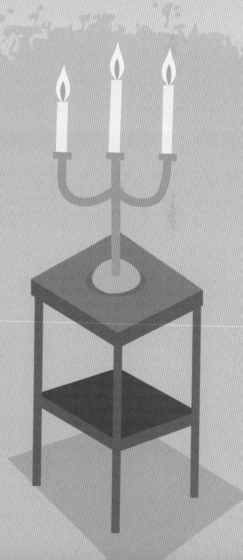

Early life

... in 30 seconds

Leonardo da Vinci was born on April 15, 1452, close to the town of Vinci, near Florence, in what we now call Italy. Although we know him as Leonardo da Vinci, his full name was Leonardo di ser Piero da Vinci. This means he was Leonardo, son of Piero from Vinci.

Leonardo's father, Piero, was a lawyer. His mother, Caterina, was a farmer's daughter. Since they weren't married, Leonardo would not have been allowed to go to university or to enter certain professions.

Little is known about Leonardo's early life. When he was very young, his father married a woman called Albiera. Leonardo may have been in the care of Caterina for the first few years, and then in the care of his father and stepmother. He had a basic education, but was often left to amuse himself. Perhaps this fueled his natural curiosity.

When Leonardo was 14, his father found him a place as an apprentice in the studio of a famous artist known as Andrea del Verrocchio. Here he would learn from the master how to be an artist and would later join a guild, an association of craftspeople.

3-second sum-up

Leonardo had a humble childhood before he became an apprentice artist at 14.

Leonardo's first painting

When Leonardo first joined Verrocchio's studio, he would have helped to mix paints and prepare canvases. One of his first known contributions to a painting is the image of an angel in Verrocchio's painting *The Baptism of Christ*. There is a story that Verrocchio was so impressed with his pupil's work that he grew ashamed of his own ability as a painter, and decided never to paint again.

When he was 14 years old, Leonardo became an apprentice artist in the studio of Andrea del Verrocchio, an important painter.

Apprentices learned many skills, including how to draw people who posed for them.

Verrocchio's studio produced artwork for wealthy clients.

Once apprentices were good enough, they helped out on real paintings for clients.

Leonardo's first known work is of an angel in Verrocchio's painting *The Baptism of Christ.*

Warring city states
... in 30 seconds

By 1482 Leonardo had left Verrocchio's studio and moved north to the city state of Milan, where he worked for a very powerful man called Ludovico Sforza, who gave him a commission to make a huge bronze horse (see page 34).

Leonardo had written to Ludovico a year before asking for work, firstly as a military engineer (see page 42) and secondly as a painter and sculptor. This was because these were violent times and Leonardo figured a military engineer would be more useful than an artist.

The violence arose because Italy was not a unified country. Instead, there were a number of different city states, each with their own rules and rulers, who often fought each other. So, although it was a time of great opportunities for a talented man such as Leonardo, life was full of danger and he needed the protection of powerful people to succeed.

For this reason, Leonardo was to spend most of his life in Milan and Florence. The Sforza family were extremely rich and employed Leonardo for nearly two decades. Florence—an arch rival of Milan—was controlled by the Medici family, who lavished money on geniuses such as Leonardo.

3-second sum-up

These were unstable times, and artists needed help from wealthy supporters.

Leonardo's Résumé!

In a letter to his future employer, Ludovico Sforza, Leonardo advertised his skills as an inventor of war machines, saying:

"... I will make covered vehicles, safe and unassailable, which will penetrate enemy ranks with their artillery and destroy the most powerful troops; the infantry may follow them without meeting obstacles or suffering damage."

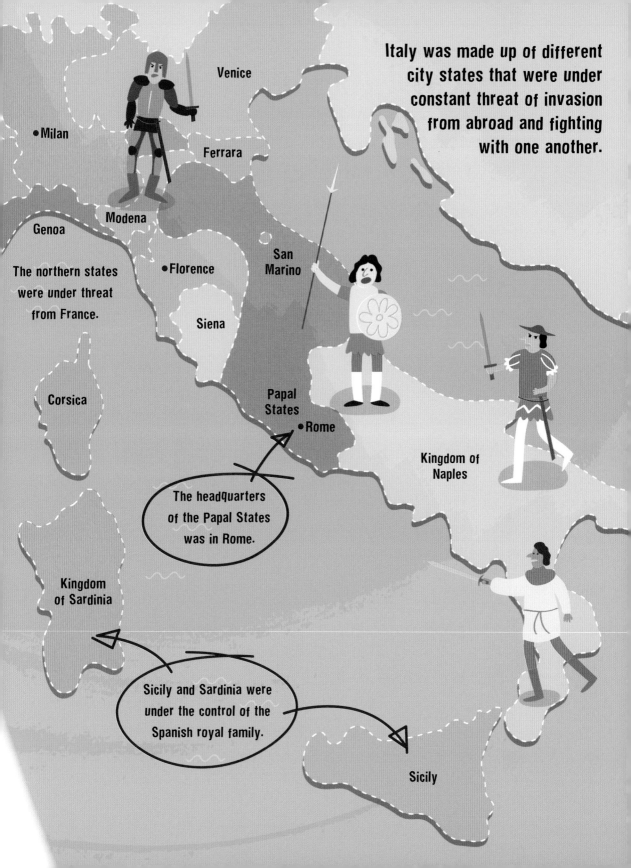

Italy was made up of different city states that were under constant threat of invasion from abroad and fighting with one another.

Venice

Milan

Ferrara

Modena

Genoa

The northern states were under threat from France.

Florence

San Marino

Siena

Corsica

Papal States

Rome

The headquarters of the Papal States was in Rome.

Kingdom of Naples

Kingdom of Sardinia

Sicily and Sardinia were under the control of the Spanish royal family.

Sicily

An original thinker
... in 30 seconds

Like any other artist who had learned their craft in a studio such as Verrocchio's, Leonardo was taught a variety of different painting techniques. But this wasn't enough for Leonardo, who was very curious— and not just about painting. He studied the world around him in a scientific way and was continually asking the question "why?"

Leonardo's investigations sometimes led him to ideas that were dangerous for the times. For example, he spent many hours researching the movement of water, which led him to the conclusion that the Bible story of Noah's Ark and the Flood could not have happened as it was described.

This was troubling for two reasons. Sometimes the Catholic church gave Leonardo a commission to depict religious topics and they would not have approved of his views. More seriously, questioning the Bible or the teachings of the Church could get you arrested—or even executed! For these reasons, he kept his views to himself, recording them in private in his journals.

Leonardo's views were so different from those of his contemporaries that his mind was described as "heretical," which means his views were generally not accepted by society at that time.

3-second sum-up

Leonardo wasn't afraid to be different.

Was Leonardo a vegetarian?

Although there is some evidence that Leonardo chose not to eat meat, we don't really know if this is true. However, in his notebooks, we learn that he felt differently about animals than did his contemporaries. For example, he believed that people should not raise animals only to kill them. An early animal activist, Leonardo also freed caged birds.

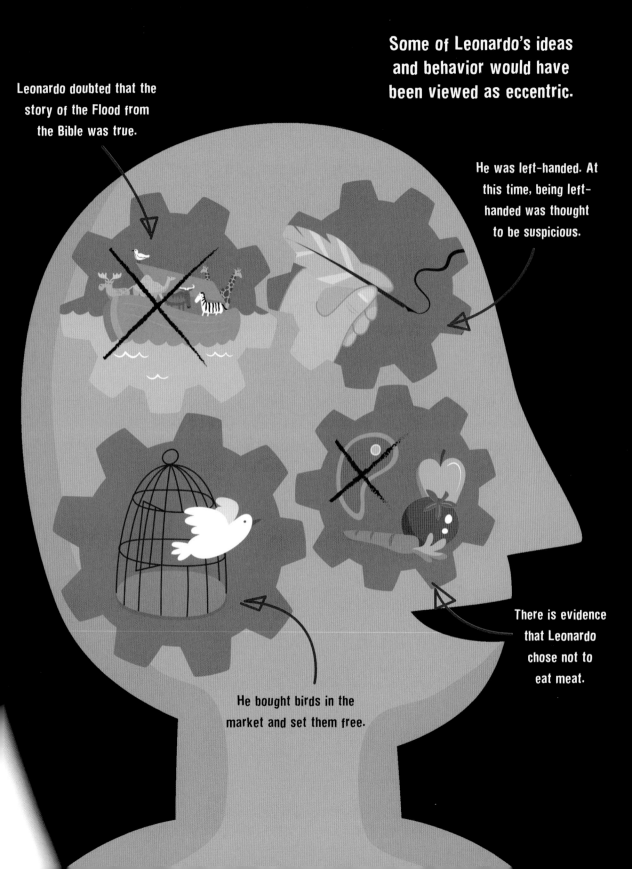

Leonardo doubted that the story of the Flood from the Bible was true.

Some of Leonardo's ideas and behavior would have been viewed as eccentric.

He was left-handed. At this time, being left-handed was thought to be suspicious.

He bought birds in the market and set them free.

There is evidence that Leonardo chose not to eat meat.

Leonardo's notebooks

... in 30 seconds

Leonardo was set to become a painter—which was what he became, but he was also much more. An avid note-taker, he filled pages and pages with his ideas, sketches, and thoughts throughout his career. Amazingly, thousands of these pages still exist and they provide a fascinating insight into the mind of a genius.

Leonardo's notebooks show the vast number of subjects his work covered. There are pages of sketches and designs that show us his knowledge of anatomy, nature, architecture, science, and math. He even wrote his shopping lists and ingredients for making paint!

Another noticeable feature is Leonardo's handwriting. The notebooks are written in Italian, which show his lack of schooling (pupils at that time were taught in Latin). Secondly, the writing is in reverse—the words are written from right to left as opposed to left to right like normal writing. Was this a way of keeping his ideas secret? Or was it because he was left-handed, and writing with a quill and ink would have been easier this way?

More often than not, these notebooks are collections of loose sheets that were put together after Leonardo's death. Today the notebooks are in museums or private collections. They tell us a lot about Leonardo.

3-second sum-up

We know about Leonardo's ideas from his notebooks.

3-minute mission Mirror writing

Start at the right-hand edge of the paper and write across the page to the left. Make sure all your letters face in the opposite direction from the way you would normally write them. Hold a mirror to the left-hand edge and your words should appear the right way around.

Artist

Perhaps the best-known fact about Leonardo is that he painted the *Mona Lisa,* which is the most famous (and the most valuable) painting in the entire world! Leonardo was a brilliant artist who developed new ways of painting that made his artwork look more realistic than anything else that was being done at the time. He wasn't just a painter, though—he was gifted at sculpting and hiding messages in his work, too!

Artist Glossary

commission When a person orders a painting or artwork from an artist, and arranges to pay him or her when the work is complete.

glaze A thinly applied, see-through layer of color that is added to dry paint. Light passes through the glaze, reflecting the underlying color, so glazed paintings look richer and colors are more intense.

foreground The part of the picture that is nearest to the observer.

horizon line In the real world, this is the line where the sky meets the Earth. In a painting, it is the eye-level line, the horizontal line that is the focus of the painting.

luminous Colors that reflect light so they look as if they are lit up from within.

master A skilled craftsperson or artist who undertakes the training of apprentices.

masterpiece A work of outstanding skill and beauty. In Leonardo's day, craftspeople and artists had to produce a masterpiece to qualify as a master of their guild.

merchant A person who buys goods, often imported from foreign lands, and sells them to others.

muted Color that is naturally soft. Bright colors can be muted by adding white or gray.

perspective A representation, in two dimensions (for example, paper), of a **three-dimensional** image as it is seen by the eye.

Renaissance A period of European history between the 14th and 17th centuries, when there were great advances in art, literature, education, exploration, and thinking.

sculpture Shaping wood, metal, stone, or other materials to make **three-dimensional** forms, such as human or animal figures.

sfumato A painting technique in which colors and tones merge gradually into each other, creating soft and hazy outlines.

shade Mixing a color with black to reduce lightness.

symbol An object that represents something else, usually an idea, a quality, or a belief.

tempera A fast-drying paint, where the color is mixed with a binding medium, usually egg yolk. Tempera paintings are very long lasting.

three-dimensional An object with height, width, and depth, like objects in the real world.

tone A color created by adding both white and black (i.e. gray) to create a more complex color.

transparent Something see-through or clear: for example, glass.

underpainting The first layer of paint on a canvas; this acts as a base for layers that are added later. Leonardo used neutral colors, such as pale gray or brown.

vanishing point In a painting, this is the point on the horizon at which parallel lines converge (meet up). As things get farther away they seem to get smaller and closer together. When they get far enough away, distances become ever smaller, forming a single point.

Oil painting
... in 30 seconds

When people looked at Leonardo's paintings, they saw far more realistic images than they had ever seen before. This was because Leonardo had developed new painting techniques and new paints.

Leonardo was one of the first artists to use paints mixed with oil. Before then, artists usually mixed their paint with egg yolk. Egg tempera paint dried very quickly, so artists had to work fast and follow a definite plan. Oil paint dries very slowly, which meant that Leonardo had more time to work on his pictures and change them as he went along.

Leonardo painted in layers, slowly adding near-transparent color glazes on top of other layers. With each layer, the overall color changed, ever so slightly. The effect was amazing—it produced delicate, almost luminous tones—but it did take ages to complete as each layer had to dry first. The layering technique is also what gives Leonardo's paintings the deep colors and richness that make them stand out.

Leonardo used another technique, too, called "sfumato," which means "to tone down." Instead of outlining the painted image, his fine shading and delicate brush strokes created soft, almost invisible, borders between colors and tones.

3-second sum-up

Leonardo developed new ways of painting.

3-minute mission Make paint

You need: • 1½ cups water • 1 cup flour • 1 cup salt • Food coloring • **Warning:** Food coloring can stain

Mix together the ingredients and divide the mixture into bowls. Add different colors to each bowl and start painting. Try adding a few drops of oil and see what difference it makes to the paint.

Leonardo built up his paintings in layers and made his own paint.

He underpainted everything with a brown wash.

He slowly added layers of lighter color.

He used many tones of the same color to suggest realistic shadows.

He made his own paints from oils, plants, rocks, and even insects.

Perspective, light, and color
... in 30 seconds

Leonardo spent many hours observing the world around him, sketching what he saw and making notes. His aim was to make his paintings mirror the real world as much as possible. His biggest challenge was how to translate the three-dimensional world into the two-dimensional (flat) pictures he was painting. To achieve his goals, he used various artistic techniques and tricks, such as perspective.

The use of light and color was important in Leonardo's work, too. He spent many hours observing the way shadows work and sketching folds of cloth to make sure that they looked as real as possible. By getting the shadows and shading right, he could suggest the weight or lightness of materials. The way light and shadow worked in his paintings and the luminosity of his painting technique was far beyond the skills of most artists of the time.

He also used neat tricks to help give his paintings depth. By using darker colors in the foreground and bluer colors in the background, he made the background seem far away—as it would be in the real world. This was revolutionary for his time.

3-second sum-up

Perspective, shading, and color make the paintings look three-dimensional.

3-minute mission Practice perspective

Draw a line in the middle of your picture. This is the horizon line — where the sky meets the land. Mark a point in the middle of the line— this is called the vanishing point. Everything you draw should get bigger as it gets farther away from this point.

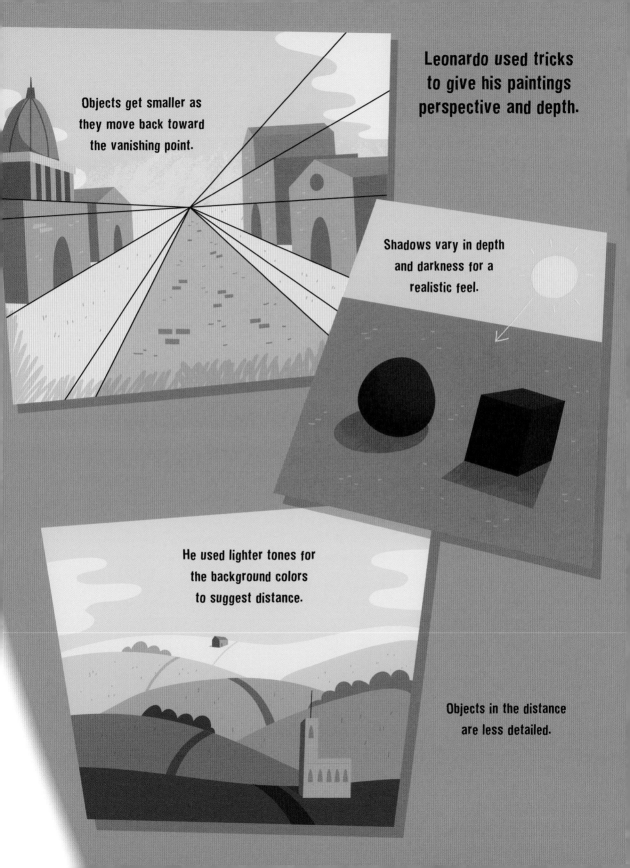

The *Mona Lisa*

... in 30 seconds

Leonardo created what is probably the most recognizable painting in the world—the *Mona Lisa*. It is a portrait of a woman, but, strangely, no one knows who she is. There have been many theories, including that it was a self-portrait of Leonardo in women's clothes! However, the most likely answer is that the painting is of a woman called Lisa Gherardini, who was married to an Italian silk merchant called Francesco del Giocondo.

Another mystery surrounding the painting is that it was never finished. While this is true of many of Leonardo's works, the *Mona Lisa* is different because Leonardo continued to work on it for many years and kept it until his death. It was clearly important to him—it's a shame we don't know why. What we do know is that the way Leonardo captured the woman's strange half-smile has fascinated people for centuries and continues to do so.

The *Mona Lisa* now hangs in the Louvre Museum in Paris, France. It is claimed that approximately six million people come to look at the painting each year! To keep it safe, the *Mona Lisa* is protected by a layer of bulletproof glass.

3-second sum-up

It's the most famous painting in the world, but we don't know who the *Mona Lisa* is.

Stolen!

On August 21, 1911, the *Mona Lisa* was stolen from the Louvre by a disguised thief called Vincenzo Peruggia who simply walked out of the gallery with the painting hidden under his artist's smock! It was recovered two years later and returned to the gallery.

Who is this woman?

Some people say this mysterious woman is named Lisa Gherardini.

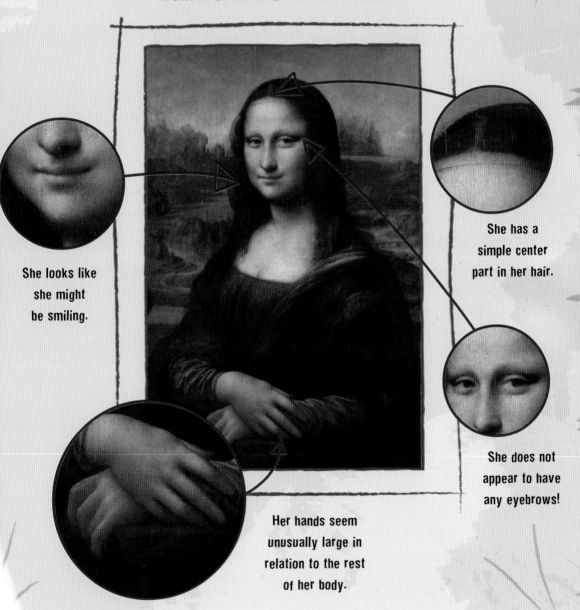

She looks like she might be smiling.

She has a simple center part in her hair.

She does not appear to have any eyebrows!

Her hands seem unusually large in relation to the rest of her body.

Symbols and secrets
... in 30 seconds

Leonardo filled his paintings with hidden meanings and symbols. A symbol is something that represents something else. In Leonardo's day, people would have recognized and understood most of the symbols in his paintings. For example, at the bottom left of his famous painting, the *Virgin of the Rocks*, Leonardo added Stars of Bethlehem, or heartsease, a plant that symbolized purity. It is there because purity is a quality associated with the Virgin Mary.

Leonardo's painting of *The Last Supper* shows Jesus and his 12 followers, the apostles, sitting at a table. The apostles are grouped in threes and there are three windows, which may represent the Holy Trinity (God, Jesus, and the Holy Spirit). Spilled salt is said to mean bad luck. In the painting the salt is spilled in front of Judas, the apostle who betrayed Jesus.

Unfortunately for us, we don't know what all of the symbols in Leonardo's paintings mean. For instance, he often painted people holding one of their hands in a strange position, pointing up into the air. This appears in quite a few of Leonardo's works, so it clearly means something. One idea is that they are pointing to where people thought heaven could be found, or maybe Leonardo just thought that it looked dramatic!

3-second sum-up

Leonardo's paintings contain many symbolic meanings and hidden messages.

3-minute mission
Make your own secret message

Create your own secret code—just like Leonardo. Choose different symbols to represent different letters such as a triangle for an "A" or a bee for a "B." Now send a secret message to your friends and see if they can understand what you are saying. You might have to give them one or two clues to help them crack the code!

Leonardo used symbols in his paintings. Here are some of the plant symbols that he used and their meanings.

PALM

Victory—palms have been symbolic since pre-Christian times.

LILY

Purity—lilies often appear in paintings of the Virgin Mary.

BEAR'S BREECHES

Resurrection—bear's breeches often grows on graves.

COLUMBINE

The Holy Spirit—the plant resembles a dove, symbol of the Holy Spirit.

CYCLAMEN

Love—because of its heart-shaped leaves.

Sculpture
... in 30 seconds

As a Renaissance artist, Leonardo was expected to be able to turn his hand to most forms of art, including sculpture. He would have learned the basic techniques when he was an apprentice in Florence in the studio of his master, Verrocchio. Later he got a commission to produce sculptures that would be the perfect showcase for his talents.

The Duke of Milan, Ludovico Sforza, hired Leonardo to build a statue of a horse, but not just any horse—this one was to be bronze and, at over 23 feet high, was to be bigger than any other horse statue in the world. Leonardo spent years making sketches and preparing his model and, in the 1490s, he made a full-size model out of clay, which he unveiled to the Duke to much fanfare.

However, the project was never completed. Leonardo got distracted by other projects and never got around to melting the bronze to make the statue. Then, in 1494, war broke out between Milan and France. Suddenly the bronze that had been reserved for the statue was needed to make cannons. The statue was never made and—worse still—the invading French troops used the clay model as a target for archery practice! A cast of Leonardo's horse statue, based on his drawings, now stands in Milan.

3-second sum-up

Leonardo designed a bronze horse statue but only completed the clay model.

3-minute mission
Make your own modeling clay

You need: • 1 cup flour • ½ cup salt • Few drops of oil • ½ cup water • Food coloring • **Warning:** Food coloring can stain

Mix all the ingredients together. If it's too wet add more flour; if it's too dry add more liquid. Divide into pieces and color with food coloring. Now start sculpting and create a masterpiece!

The bronze intended for the statue was used to make cannons.

Leonardo spent years planning his horse sculpture. He finally made the clay model, which was then destroyed!

The final statue was never made.

The model was destroyed by the French to annoy the Duke of Milan.

French archers used the model for target practice.

Inventor Glossary

automata Mechanical figures or devices that are designed to act automatically, without someone controlling their movements.

biography An account of a person's life and work. Giorgio Vasari wrote a famous biography of Leonardo in the mid-16th century.

catapult A device that is used to hurl missiles with great force over long distances.

codex A book, made up of loose leaves of paper, that is handwritten, rather than printed.

clockwork A mechanism that is driven by springs and gear wheels.

cog The tiny teeth that fit together on a series of gear wheels, making the wheels turn.

crossbow A type of bow that is fixed to a wooden support, or stock. A lever is attached to the stock and when it is released the arrow is fired with great speed and accuracy.

gear A wheel with teeth along its outer rim that fit together with other wheels' teeth. Gears transmit motion and are seen in many inventions, from clocks to cars.

kingdom A country, state, or territory that is ruled by a king or queen.

master A skilled craftsperson or artist who is responsible for training apprentices.

parachute A lightweight cloth that fills with air and is designed to slow down the motion of any attached objects; for example, a person falling through the atmosphere.

pendulum A weight that is hung from a fixed point, also called a pivot, and that swings freely.

pulley A simple machine that uses grooved wheels and a rope to raise, lower, or move a load.

Renaissance A period of European history between the 14th and 17th centuries, when there were great advances in art, literature, exploration, and thinking.

replica An exact copy or model of something, often built on a smaller scale than the original.

republic A state that is governed by the people, or by the rulers who they elect, rather than by a king or queen.

spring A device, usually coiled (or twisted), that can be pressed or pushed, but which will return to its original shape when released.

tank A heavily armored fighting vehicle that can be used to protect the soldiers inside.

41

War machines

... in 30 seconds

As the kingdoms and republics of Italy clashed with each other for power and territory, Leonardo made himself useful to wealthy clients by inventing machines that could be used in war for attack and defense.

Leonardo had a simple trick up his sleeve to get his designs noticed—he made them as big and as impressive as possible. His idea for a crossbow doesn't show a handheld weapon like the other crossbows of the time. Leonardo's crossbow was huge—approximately 67 feet across—and needed wheels to move it. The string was pulled back by a man winding a crank (a kind of handle) and it could fire rocks, like a catapult.

Leonardo also drew designs for cannons that could fire multiple cannon balls that would explode individually, and for cannons with more than one barrel. There were drawings of a covered ladder that could be wheeled up to city walls to keep invading soldiers safe from arrow-fire and he drew carts with revolving blades for hacking down the enemy.

He also invented an armored car that was capable of moving in any direction, which was equipped with a large number of weapons.

3-second sum-up

Leonardo designed war machines for wealthy customers.

Did Leonardo deliberately make mistakes?

There is a theory that Leonardo's war machines were designed with flaws in them so that they would never be used. Indeed, some of the flaws are so obvious, it is strange that Leonardo didn't notice them. He once described war as a "beastly madness," leading some people to believe that he was a pacifist.

Wonders on wheels
... in 30 seconds

The Renaissance world was powered by hooves. If you wanted to get somewhere fast, you rode a horse. If you had heavy things to move, you used a horse and cart or an ox. To a problem-solver like Leonardo this was a challenge—how could transportation be improved? It led him to come up with a number of ideas, including something that resembled a car!

Leonardo's "car" was a self-propelled cart. He never got around to making it, and it took another 500 years after his death before someone decided to build it using his sketches. Amazingly, the cart worked.

The cart was powered by two coiled springs that pushed it along as the springs unwound—a bit like a clockwork toy. The cart could only travel short distances and although it could steer, the angle had to be set before the cart moved. There was a brake in case of emergencies!

Although Leonardo didn't invent anything as complex as the first true car, he made an imaginative leap, realizing that transportation did not need to be powered by animals or humans or the forces of nature. It would be hundreds of years before everyone else caught up with his idea.

3-second sum-up

Leonardo invented a self-propelled vehicle hundreds of years before cars existed.

3-minute mission
Make you own self-powered vehicle

You need: • Spool • Rubber band • A toothpick • Adhesive tape • Pencil

Thread the rubber band through the spool. Tie one end over the toothpick so that it lies flat against the spool and secure with tape. Slide the pencil into the other end so three-quarters is sticking out at one end (make sure the rubber band isn't too loose). Now wind the pencil around and let your "wheel" roll away.

Leonardo investigated the use of mechanical power hundreds of years before anyone else.

The humble horse and cart had been used for thousands of years.

Leonardo's cart was self-propelled.

His invention could steer, brake, and move under its own power!

Karl Benz invented the first true automobile in 1885.

Taking flight
... in 30 seconds

Leonardo was fascinated by the idea of flight. He studied the way birds took to the air and made scientific observations that were centuries ahead of their time. However, what really intrigued Leonardo was the idea that a person could fly, and he sketched ideas of how this might happen.

Leonardo drew plans for a helicopter. He based his idea on the Archimedes screw—an ancient Greek invention for moving water— on which modern-day screws are based. Leonardo correctly assumed that the way the screw was angled would provide the lift needed to pull the helicopter into the air. Infuriatingly, he didn't really know how the screw would be powered!

What goes up must come down, and, in case of flying emergencies, Leonardo invented a parachute. This was one invention that really did work. A replica was built and tested in the year 2000 and the brave volunteer who tried it survived a jump from a height of 9,800 feet!

3-second sum-up

Leonardo's ideas for flying machines were ahead of their time.

3-minute mission Make a helicopter

You need: • Long, thin strip of paper • Paper clip

Fold the strip of paper in half, so that it is half the length. Attach the paper clip to the folded end. Fold one of the strips at the other end over to the right, and the other strip over to the left to make a "T" shape. Now throw it high in the air and watch how it spins as it falls—just like a helicopter.

Leonardo's dreams of flying machines were based on scientific observations.

Leonardo's plans for a helicopter were based on the Archimedes screw.

Leonardo invented a parachute made of linen cloth held open by rigid wooden poles.

Much of Leonardo's work on flight is now in the *Codex Atlanticus*, a 12-volume collection of his notes and drawings.

Automata

... in 30 seconds

Leonardo's ideas on mechanical movement went well beyond transportation. If you think that robots are a modern invention, think again. Leonardo designed, and actually made, working models that could move. Naturally these models caused quite a stir and impressed King Francis I of France so much that he invited Leonardo to come and work for him.

The correct name for models that can move is automata. There are reports that Leonardo made at least three models of lions that could move in one way or another. His first model was made in around 1509 and could rise up on its hind legs. His second model, which was built around 1515, was a more impressive affair. It could walk, wag its tail, move its head from side to side, and open its jaws. When King Francis was invited to touch it with his sword, the lion's body opened up to reveal fresh lilies—a symbol of the French royal family—inside. No wonder the King was impressed.

Inside the lion were cogs, gears, pulleys, and a pendulum that, unsurprisingly for Leonardo, were all well ahead of their time. The designs inside his journals are all that are left of Leonardo's lions today, but a modern-day replica proved that his lion could work.

3-second sum-up

Leonardo's automata brought acclaim and even a new job offer in a foreign country.

King Francis I of France

King Francis was Leonardo's last patron. In 1516, impressed by Leonardo's genius, he invited him to come and work for him in France. Leonardo was given a home and a huge salary to be the King's painter, engineer, and architect, a position he held until his death in 1519. Leonardo brought more than his talents to France—he also brought the *Mona Lisa*, which is why it is displayed in France today rather than in Italy.

Leonardo's ingenious automata amazed everyone who saw them.

The lion could sit down, stand up, and move its arms and head.

The lion had all of its moving parts inside the body.

Leonardo built a robot knight in about 1495.

The knight was reconstructed in 1996, and it worked!

A series of pulleys and gears enabled it to move.

Musical inventions

... in 30 seconds

The Italian artist and historian Giorgio Vasari (1511–1574) wrote a biography of Leonardo. He tells us that Leonardo was a gifted musician who could play any stringed instrument. We know that Leonardo could definitely play the lira da braccio, which looked like a seven-stringed violin. He probably learned his musical skills from his master Verrocchio, who owned a guitar-like instrument called a lute. Some people say that Leonardo invented the violin, but nobody has been able to prove this.

Not only did Leonardo play instruments, but he made them as well. He once made a lyre (a small harp) for Ludovico Sforza, the Duke of Milan. Leonardo's lyre was remarkable because not only was it in the shape of a horse's skull, it was also made of silver. Apparently it sounded better than a normal lyre, too. Needless to say, the Duke was very pleased with his gift!

Leonardo also combined a stringed instrument with a keyboard to create a "viola organista." Although Leonardo never built one himself, his design has been tried out since and been shown to work.

3-second sum-up

Leonardo played, invented, and made musical instruments.

3-minute mission Create a musical instrument

You need: • Rubber bands of different thicknesses • Small cardboard box with a lid • Scissors • Pen

Stretch the rubber bands over the box (with the lid removed). Pluck the bands and listen to the different sounds they make. Try cutting out a large hole in the lid and putting it on top of the box, just like a guitar. Now raise the rubber bands by pushing a pen underneath. Does it sound different?

A gifted musician, Leonardo also invented several musical instruments.

The harpsichord-viola was a keyboard that was designed to be played while walking.

As this machine was pushed along, the turning wheels propelled levers, which played the drums.

The horse-head lyre was the perfect gift to impress the Duke of Milan!

Leonardo played the lira da braccio, which resembled a violin.

Leonardo drew people following the exact proportions decided by the ancient Roman writer Marcus Vitruvius.

The distance from the elbow to the tip of the middle finger is one-quarter of the person's height.

The length of the hand is one-tenth of a person's height.

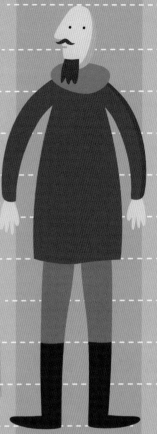

Ears start at the height of the eyebrows and finish at the end of the nose.

The width of a person's outstretched arms matches their height.

Drawing faces
... in 30 seconds

Leonardo was fascinated by human faces. He would tell his students to carry a notebook with them when they were out and about so they could draw the human body in motion and observe the faces and facial expressions of the people around them. It was advice he followed himself and his own notebooks are filled with pages and pages of sketches of people—particularly their heads.

Some of the sketches of heads in Leonardo's books were probably ideas he was preparing for other paintings. These are called preparatory sketches. Others are drawings of people who had caught his eye, or what we call caricatures—pictures where the facial features are exaggerated. In some sketches Leonardo depicted people suffering from illness. In one of Leonardo's sketches, even though they are caricatures, doctors claim they can tell what illnesses each character is suffering from.

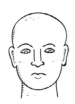

Sometimes Leonardo used his art to get back at people. For example, there is a story that the face of Judas in his painting of *The Last Supper* is based on the Prior of the monastery who commissioned the artwork. Leonardo got so fed up with the Prior asking when the painting would be finished he used the Prior's face as the man who betrayed Jesus!

3-second sum-up

Leonardo made countless sketches of heads to perfect his art.

3-minute mission Make your own caricature

Try drawing a quick caricature of a friend or even of yourself. Exaggerate the facial features. If they have big eyes, make the ones in your picture really big, or if they have a small nose, make it tiny on your caricature. Look at the shape of their head—is there any way of exaggerating that? The trick is not to go too far over the top or it won't look like the person you're drawing.

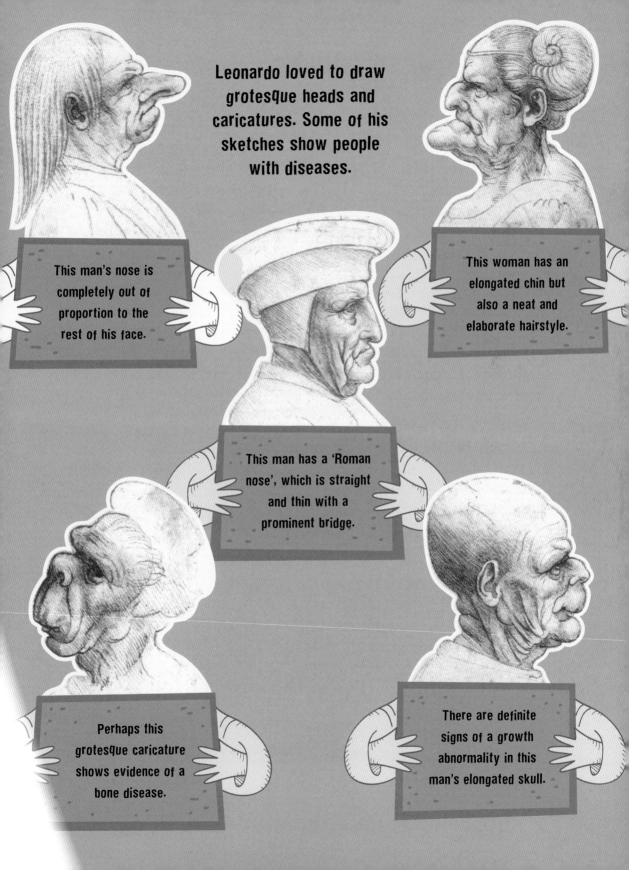

Leonardo loved to draw grotesque heads and caricatures. Some of his sketches show people with diseases.

This man's nose is completely out of proportion to the rest of his face.

This woman has an elongated chin but also a neat and elaborate hairstyle.

This man has a 'Roman nose', which is straight and thin with a prominent bridge.

Perhaps this grotesque caricature shows evidence of a bone disease.

There are definite signs of a growth abnormality in this man's elongated skull.

Accurate anatomy
... in 30 seconds

Part of the reason why Leonardo's paintings and drawings of people looked so realistic was that he understood how the human body was put together. His general curiosity and love of science led him to discover how each part of the body worked—not just on the outside, but on the inside, too.

Of course there were no such things as X-rays when Leonardo was around. To find out what was going on under the skin, he had to attend autopsies. An autopsy is when a dead body is cut open and investigated to find out why the person died. This practice was regarded with suspicion at the time, but it was allowed at hospitals and medical schools. Not only did Leonardo watch autopsies, he also conducted them himself.

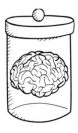

Although this might seem gruesome, Leonardo was carrying out vital research. He sketched everything he saw and may have been planning to publish his findings. As with many of his plans, his work in this area was never finished and remained unpublished. However, his sketches show he understood how tendons and blood vessels worked, and knew the role of joints, organs, and muscles within the body. His work in this field was years ahead of its time.

3-second sum-up

Leonardo's anatomical drawings were accurate and ground breaking.

Dissection!

Leonardo claimed that he cut up more than 30 bodies in his lifetime. But where did he get them? Often they were the bodies of poor people who had died from illness, or executed criminals. Most of these bodies were men. Although Leonardo did study some women, he had fewer opportunities to look at female corpses than male corpses, so his studies of women weren't quite as accurate.

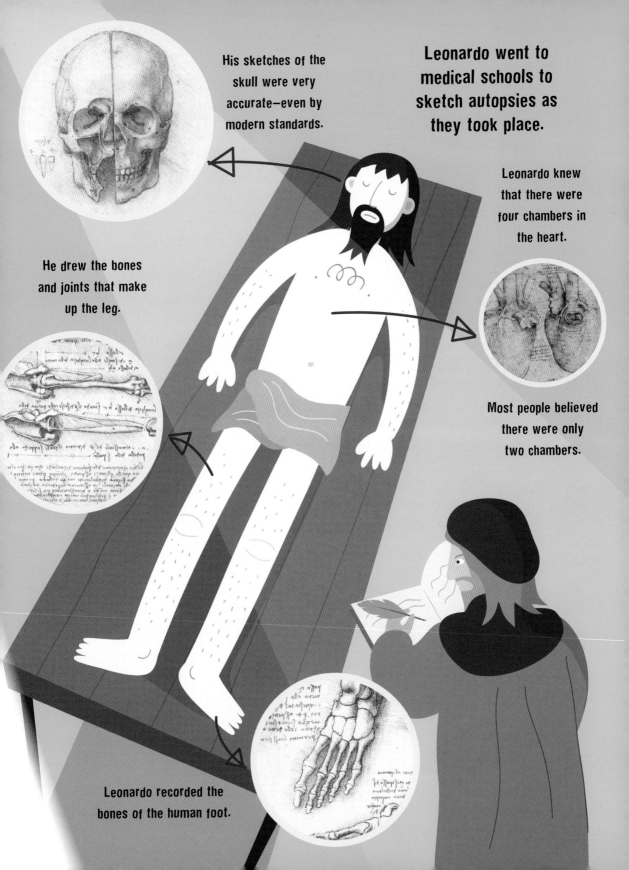

His sketches of the skull were very accurate—even by modern standards.

Leonardo went to medical schools to sketch autopsies as they took place.

Leonardo knew that there were four chambers in the heart.

He drew the bones and joints that make up the leg.

Most people believed there were only two chambers.

Leonardo recorded the bones of the human foot.

How the eye works
... in 30 seconds

Leonardo wrote that "the eye embraces the beauty of the whole world." He meant that if you looked carefully enough you would see all of nature's wonders. Yet Leonardo was also fascinated by how people could see, so he studied the inner workings of the eye.

He made some great advances on what had already been discovered and recorded, but his methods might make you squeamish—he cut up human eyes from dead bodies. He didn't always get everything right. For example, he believed that the lens (the part that focuses) was round instead of oval. This might be because the eye is filled with a jelly-like substance that spills out when the eye is cut open, which may have made getting the details correct a bit tricky. Leonardo wrote about how to get around this problem, but he may not have tried out his ideas.

Leonardo realized that when an image passes through the pupil it is flipped upside down, just like in a pinhole camera. But Leonardo didn't get the next part right. He thought that the eye would then flip the image again before it reached the brain. It would be many decades before it was discovered that it is the brain and not the eye that turns the image the right-side up!

3-second sum-up

Leonardo understood more about how the eye works than anyone before him.

3-minute mission How to make a pinhole camera

You need: • Shoe box • Scissors • Phillips screwdriver or awl • Thin wax paper • An adult helper

Make a large, square hole at one end of the box and cover it in wax paper. At the opposite end make a small circular hole. Point the hole at an object and you will see it reflected (upside down) on the wax paper. Put a cloth over your head and you will see the image more clearly. Painting the inside of the box black will also help make the image clearer.

Leonardo's theory of how vision works was only half correct.

He realized that the image is flipped when it enters the eye...

...but he thought it got flipped again at the back...

...and went to the brain right-side up.

We now know that's not what happens.

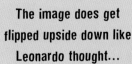

The image does get flipped upside down like Leonardo thought...

...but it's the brain's job to flip it right-side up again.

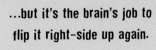

Scientist and mathematician

Leonardo was fascinated by science and used math to explore how nature worked, from the way leaves grew on plants to the way the Moon seemed to shine. He used math in his art, too, drawing his figures and buildings using geometry and perspective. His scientific studies also led him to question whether the world was much older than was thought— a very radical idea for the time.

Scientist and mathematician
Glossary

earthshine The glow that can be seen over the shadowed part of a crescent moon, caused by reflected light from Earth.

fossils The remains of plants or animals that are preserved in rock. Fossils are more than 10,000 years old and represent the ancestors of plants or animals, some of which can still be found today.

fractal A shape in which a small part of it has a similar (but not necessarily identical) appearance to the full shape.

geology The study of Earth, including how it was made, of what it is made, and how it has changed over time.

geometry The area of mathematics that deals with points, lines, shapes, and space. Plane geometry is about flat shapes, circles, and triangles. Solid geometry is about solid shapes, such as spheres and cubes.

muted Color that is naturally soft. Bright colors can be muted by adding white or gray.

perspective A representation, in two dimensions (for example, a picture on paper), of a **three-dimensional** image as it is seen by the eye.

sedimentary rock Rock formed from the debris (sand, stones, mud) that settles at the bottom of lakes.

Solar System Our Sun and everything that travels around it, such as planets and moons. The Solar System is oval, or elliptical, and is always in motion.

telescope An instrument that uses lenses to see objects that are far away; for example, planets and stars.

tetrahedron A flat-sided solid object with four faces.

three-dimensional An object with height, width, and depth, like objects in the real world.

tone A color created by adding both white and black (i.e., gray) to create a more complex color.

topology The study of shapes, in particular the properties that don't change when shapes are twisted or stretched or knotted.

transparent Something see-through or clear; for example, glass.

Universe theories

... in 30 seconds

During Leonardo's time, people had different ideas about how the universe worked. For example, it was claimed that Earth was the center of what we now know as the Solar System. To be fair, people did not have the tools to study the night sky properly, but that didn't stop Leonardo from coming up with better theories!

Many thought the Moon shone with its own light, but Leonardo was sure that the Moon was actually reflecting light back from the Sun—which it does. He wasn't completely correct; Leonardo thought the Sun's light was bouncing off water that he believed covered most of the Moon's surface.

Renaissance people believed that the Sun wasn't hot because it wasn't the same yellow as fire. Leonardo knew that it was hot— his notebooks record him comparing the Sun to the color of bronze when it is melted in a furnace and is at its hottest. He also guessed correctly that the Sun generated its own power.

Some people even think that Leonardo made designs for the first-ever telescope in his notebooks. Just think what discoveries he might have made had he ever built one!

3-second sum-up

Leonardo solved some of the mysteries of space.

3-minute mission Quick quiz

Which of these statements about Leonardo are true and which are false?

1 He thought the Moon had an atmosphere.
2 He knew the Moon didn't shine.
3 He believed that Earth traveled around the Sun.
4 He invented a telescope to study the stars.
5 He made drawings of the Moon in his notebooks.

Answers on page 96.

Leonardo used mathematics and careful observation to crack a mystery: does the Moon shine with its own light?

The unlit part of a crescent moon sometimes shines faintly at sunrise or sunset.

When sunlight is reflected from Earth to the unlit part of the Moon's surface, it is called earthshine.

Earthshine is reflected twice— once off Earth's surface and once off the Moon's surface.

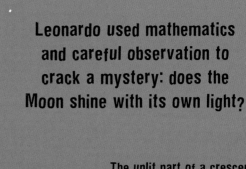

Growing patterns
... in 30 seconds

Leonardo spent many hours sketching and studying plants. The result of all this work was that when he included plants in his paintings—whether they were symbolic or not—they were so accurate that we can still recognize them today. Yet Leonardo was doing more than practicing how to draw plants; he was also making scientific studies.

Leonardo combined his many interests to make incredibly lifelike drawings. He used his knowledge of light to show how different leaves look depending on how much light is reflecting on them and how far away they are. He also described how the gaps between leaves disappear the farther away they are.

Leonardo also tried to apply his own and other people's mathematical rules to how plants grow. He believed that the thickness of a tree trunk was equal to the thickness of all the branches that grew from it. It turns out that this is not always true; but when scientists tested this theory, they discovered that trees that matched Leonardo's ideal lasted longer when buffeted by high winds than trees that didn't.

3-second sum-up

Leonardo studied plants with a scientific eye as well as an artistic one.

3-minute mission Plant finder

Find leaves from four different plants and draw them or rub them with charcoal. Follow Leonardo's example and examine the leaves closely. What patterns can you see? Can you see lines of symmetry, or spiral shapes in the way the petals or leaves are growing?

Leonardo's scientific study of plants led him to believe that they grew following mathematical rules.

Trees can withstand wind better if the thickness of their trunk is equal to the thickness of their branches.

Leonardo knew that leaves and petals grew in a spiral pattern following the same mathematical rule.

Geometric patterns
... in 30 seconds

Mathematics might seem like the total opposite of art, but not in Leonardo's mind. By his early forties, he was obsessed with mathematics, in particular areas such as perspective and geometry. He enjoyed advancing his own understanding of the subject and he also incorporated his knowledge into his paintings—for example, the *Mona Lisa*'s face is based on an arrangement of triangles and parallel lines.

Some people claim that Leonardo's notebooks contain early examples of fractals. These are complex, recurring designs that—in theory—can continue forever. Leonardo certainly sketched things like this, such as spreading patterns of transparent, three-dimensional cubes. These would have been fairly tricky to draw, but nowhere near as difficult as the complex geometric shapes he also created, such as tetrahedrons!

Knots were another branch of mathemathics that interested Leonardo. Leonardo made sketches of them and even painted one for the Duke of Milan. This was no small work; his painting of tree branches intertwining and tied by a rope covered an entire ceiling. It was math and nature combined—pure Leonardo.

3-second sum-up

Leonardo was fascinated by geometry and perspective.

3-minute mission Points of view

Sometimes your eyes can deceive you, and Leonardo enjoyed playing with optical illusions. See for yourself. Draw two lines the same length, one above the other. At the ends of one line, draw arrow shapes pointing outward. On the other line, draw arrow shapes pointing inward, with the points of the arrow touching the ends. It will look like the first arrow is longer than the second.

Leonardo used math and geometry in his drawings and paintings.

This design reflects his fascination with knots and the science now known as topology.

A fine grasp of geometry allowed him to create complex three-dimensional shapes.

He used mathematical shapes when drawing faces and bodies.

Visionary

As far as Leonardo was concerned, the world was a puzzle that he was desperate to solve. This was especially true when he was looking at the environment where he lived. Towns were crowded, cramped, and disease-ridden, so he designed towns that were spacious and airy. Rivers were barriers that stopped people from moving around, so he invented bridges that could be put up anywhere. Both town and country could be made orderly and he was the one to do it.

Visionary
Glossary

contour Imaginary lines on a map that join points of equal height. They are used to indicate hills and mountains.

counterweight A weight that is equal to the weight of a load, so that it balances the load. Its purpose is to make lifting heavy loads easier and more efficient.

current The water moving in a river or a sea. Rivers that have a lot of water and travel steeply downhill can be fast-flowing and are said to have strong currents.

hydraulics A branch of science or engineering concerned with the use of liquids to perform mechanical tasks; for example, delivering energy through pumps and pistons.

illegitimate A historical term to describe a child born to parents who are not married.

odometer An instrument that measures the distance traveled by a vehicle. The ancient Romans invented a chariot that used a series of cogs and gears to measure the number of wheel revolutions in a mile. As each mile was completed, a pebble dropped into a box.

patron A person who gives money to an artist or musician or to a charity.

pulley A simple machine that uses grooved wheels and a rope to raise, lower, or move a load.

Renaissance A period of European history between the 14th and 17th centuries, when there were great advances in art, literature, exploration, and thinking.

sanitation The facilities that ensure that the health and wellbeing of people is protected. This means providing ways of disposing of human waste safely.

scaffolding A temporary structure that is built against the side of a building (or inside tall buildings such as cathedrals) and which is designed to support

people working on construction, repair, or decoration.

sediment Solid material that is moved to another location by wind, ice, or water. It can consist of rocks and minerals as well as the remains of plants and animals.

symmetry When one half of an object is the mirror image of the other half.

Buildings and cities
... in 30 seconds

Towns and cities in Renaissance Europe were often sprawling and chaotic. Narrow streets were blocked by people and carts, filth piled up in streets, and houses crowded in on each other. People were packed in together and disease spread rapidly. Leonardo strived for order and beauty, so he set his mind to planning beautiful buildings.

Leonardo drew plans for two-story buildings that had shops on the ground floor and living quarters above. This wasn't a new idea—the ancient Romans had done that more than a thousand years earlier—but Leonardo's designs were graceful and elegant. He also drew plans for churches and cathedrals, which looked beautiful and also worked out mathematically, with pleasing symmetry and geometric shapes. Leonardo turned his talent to designing fortresses, too, with rounded towers and sloping walls to deflect cannon balls.

Leonardo drew plans for his ideal city. He realized that good sanitation was the key to a healthy city. Canals would be used for transportation and to take away rubbish. There would be large open spaces, wide streets, and a two-level road system. The lower level would be for carts and animals, while the top level would be reserved for gentlemen and ladies. Clean air would circulate through the streets via a system of windmills.

3-second sum-up

Leonardo designed buildings and planned cities.

Constructive thinking

Leonardo thought hard about how his buildings would actually be constructed. His journals show sketches of scaffolding for use when making staircases or archways. It could be argued that it is easy to draw beautiful buildings, but a different matter to actually build them—which Leonardo never did. Yet most people would agree that Leonardo would probably find a way to overcome any problems.

Leonardo took his ideas about town planning from ancient cities and improved on them.

Squares were meeting places and the open spaces helped fresh air to move around.

ifferent roads had different urposes to keep them free of traffic jams.

Leonardo's buildings were meant to be beautiful as well as practical.

Building bridges
... in 30 seconds

In addition to all his other inventions, Leonardo also tried his hand at designing bridges. His sketches show a range of different structures from simple to the very grand. Leonardo used different techniques and ideas to overcome practical problems.

Leonardo was especially good at designing temporary bridges that were easy to put together and light to transport—ideal for an army on the march that needed to cross a river. Possibly his most ingenious bridge was also his simplest. It was made from a few logs with notches cut into them. The clever part was that it was self-supporting and didn't need to be fastened together. What's more, the greater the weight on the bridge the stronger it became—simply genius!

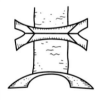

A more ambitious temporary bridge was designed for the Duke of Milan. The revolving bridge could be built on one side of a river, and when complete, swung across to the opposite bank using a clever system of ropes, pulleys, and counterweights. Leonardo's grandest bridge, a 790-foot single span across the Golden Horn in Turkey, was not built at the time. In 2001 Leonardo's design was used to make a shorter footbridge in Norway—and it was a success!

3-second sum-up

Leonardo's bridges were original and practical.

3-minute mission Bridge strength

You need: • Two pieces of card • Two thick books • Coins

Place the books a short distance apart and lay the card across the top. See how many coins you can place on the middle of the card before the bridge collapses. Now bend the second piece of card to make an arch shape and place it underneath the bridge. How many coins can the bridge hold now?

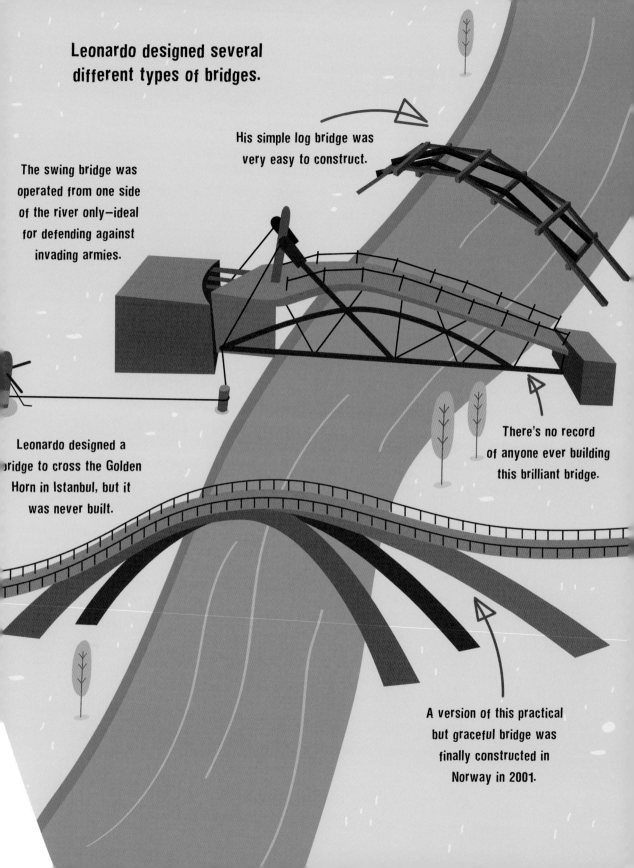

**Leonardo designed several
different types of bridges.**

His simple log bridge was
very easy to construct.

The swing bridge was
operated from one side
of the river only—ideal
for defending against
invading armies.

Leonardo designed a
bridge to cross the Golden
Horn in Istanbul, but it
was never built.

There's no record
of anyone ever building
this brilliant bridge.

A version of this practical
but graceful bridge was
finally constructed in
Norway in 2001.

Water world
... in 30 seconds

Water fascinated Leonardo—both how it moved and how it could be moved. He spent a lifetime studying streams and rivers. He conducted experiments to measure river flow and currents, and understood how moving water cut channels through rock and how sediment built up. Leonardo used this knowledge to help him design countless plans and machines.

Leonardo was well aware of the power of moving water and developed machines that made use of this source of energy. He designed saws based on hydraulics and a machine for making iron rods as well as pumps that could move water up a tower or draw water from under the ground. He also drew sketches for submarines and early diving suits.

One of Leonardo's most ambitious projects was to connect the inland city of Florence to the sea using both the River Arno and new canals designed by him. Connecting Florence to the sea would enable more trade, increasing the power and wealth of the city. Work started on the grand canal but, believe it or not, a flood destroyed all the work that had been completed.

3-second sum-up

The power of moving water fascinated Leonardo.

Locked tight

There is one Leonardo invention you can still see in operation today. Canals have what are called lock gates, which allow boats to move between canals built at slightly different levels. Leonardo developed a new kind of lock gate that used the power of the water to keep it closed. It was so successful that a version of it is still in use in modern-day locks.

Leonardo died nearly 500 years ago, but his legacy lives on.

me experts think that is is Leonardo's self-trait, painted when he s about 60 years old.

Other experts believe that this man could be Leonardo's father—or someone else. No one is sure.

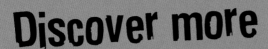

Discover more

BOOKS

Leonardo da Vinci: The Genius Who Defined the Renaissance
by John Phillips
National Geographic Society, 2008

Leonardo da Vinci
by John Malam
QED Publishing, 2014

Avoid Being Leonardo da Vinci
by Jacqueline Morley
Book House, 2014

Eyewitness Guide: Leonardo da Vinci
by Andrew Langley
Dorling Kindersley, 2006

Junior Leonardo da Vinci
by Roberta Holt
CreateSpace Independent Publishing Platform, 2013

ONLINE VIDEOS

*http://kids.britannica.com/
comptons/art-193902/Leonardo-da-
Vinci-a-genius-in-several-fields-was-
the?&articleTypeId=31*

*http://www.neok12.com/video/
History-of-Europe/
zX730d645c0f7a6907700563.htm*

WEBSITES

Complete works
http://www.leonardoda-vinci.org/

British Library
http://www.bl.uk/onlinegallery/
features/leonardo/leonardo.html

The Metropolitan Museum of Art
http://www.metmuseum.org/toah/
hd/leon/hd_leon.htm

Paintings and life
http://www.leonardodavinci.net/

Although every endeavor has been made by the publisher to ensure that all content from these websites is of the highest quality and is age appropriate, we strongly advise that Internet access be supervised by a responsible adult.

Index

Answers

Page 68 Quick quiz

1. He thought the Moon had an atmosphere. True
2. He knew the Moon didn't shine. True
3. He believed that Earth traveled round the Sun. True
4. He invented a telescope to study the stars. False
5. He made drawings of the Moon in his notebooks. True